MW00883596

California Tax Lien and Deed Investing Book

Buying Real Estate Investment Property for Beginners

By Brian Mahoney

Disclaimer Notice

This book was written as a guide and for information, educational and entertainment purposes only. No warranties of any kind are expressed or implied.

Readers acknowledge that the author is not engaging in the rendering of legal, financial, medical or professional advice, and the information in this book is not meant to take the place of any professional advice. If advice is needed in any of these fields, you are advised to seek the services of a professional.

While the author has attempted to make the information in this book as accurate as possible, no guarantee is given as to the accuracy or currency of any individual item. Laws and procedures related to business, health and well being are constantly changing.

Therefore, in no event shall the author of this book be liable for any special, indirect, or consequential damages or any damages whatsoever in connection with the use of the information herein provided.

Dedication

I would like to dedicate this book to my sister Rachel. Who listens to all my business ideas no , matter how long I go on talking about it.

Table of Contents

Section 1: 7
Tax Sale Property Overview.................................7
PART 1:...8
Benefits of Investing in Tax Property in California 8
PART 2:...15
Tax Lien and Deed Investing 15
Section 2: 26
Secrets to Finding Discount Investment Property in California.....26
Part 1:...28
California Real Estate Agents................................28
Part 2:...33
Instant Access to a Ton of Discount Investment Property 33
Part 3:...40
 Wholesale Real Estate......................................40
Section 3:...52
How To Rehab Investment Property.........................52
Part 1:...53
California Handymen 53
Part 2:...56
 A step by step guide to Rehabbing Real Estate...........56
Section 4: 71
Fast Sale House Flipping......................................71
Part 1: 72
California Photographers.......................................72
Part 2: 76
House Flipping...76
Part 3: 84
How to Sell Your Investment Property Fast!...............84
Section 5: 93
Conclusion...93

Section 1:

Tax Sale Property Overview

PART 1:

Benefits of Investing in Tax Property in California

INTRODUCTION

California can be an amazing place to be a real estate investor. California has amazing weather, Hollywood Stars, a huge demand for housing, and real estate that can appreciate like crazy. It is the biggest state by population with a diverse economy that favors a strong rental market.

Investing in California tax deed properties can offer several benefits.

Here are just a few...

Lower Entry Costs:

Real estate sold at California tax default auctions often sell way below market value. This can provide investors with the opportunity to come into the real estate investing market at a much lower cost than if the property was purchased by standard means. Some government properties may even be eligible for a Title 1 loan that may be used to finance permanent property improvements that protect or improve the basic livability or utility of all types of properties.

Less Competition:

Currently high interest rates and inflation is sidelining competition when it comes to tax default auctions. In addition, many people simply don't even know there is such a thing as government auctions for real estate. Real Estate agents and companies are all over TV promoting their services. The government, however, usually does not run TV ads announcing such auctions, and in most cases the law simply allows for a small ad in a newspaper or some official bulletin or website. So most people start their house hunting with a Realtor.

Property Value Appreciation:

Property prices in California are known to increase dramatically in a relatively short period of time. Investing in tax deed property purchased at a deep discount is a great way to get a great return on investment in a market that consistently has high appreciation.

As with any business there can be downfalls.

You should also consider seeking advice from legal and financial professionals. Additionally, you should also let the information in this book assist you to create a clear investment strategy and know your risk tolerance and learn to make informed decisions.

Now lets take a look at what is going to be covered in this book, to help get you started in, investing in tax sale property:

Section 1:
Tax Sale Property Overview

Section 2:
Secrets to finding discount investment property in your state

Section 3:
How to Rehab investment property

Section 4:
Fast Sale House Flipping

Section 5:
Conclusion

Over 40 years ago, I was fortunate enough to begin my real estate investing journey by attending a Real Estate Seminar in Virginia Beach, Virginia. It was hosted by the then, legendary real estate investor Dave Del Dotto! I purchased his course.
My co-workers at the Post Office laughed at me. I STUDIED IT INSIDE and out. **Take Action.**

I purchased a single family home, well under market value because of a foundation problem. I hired a handyman to fix it and a top rated real estate agent to sell it. Two months later at closing, I was handed a check that was the equivalent my full year's salary as a Postal Worker. The laughing at work stopped, and the requests to be my partner in real estate deals began. **Take Action.**

During that time there was a retired man who also attended one of Dave's Seminars. At the end of the seminar he said...

"Dave, I love all this information, and would love to get started in real estate investing... However I figure, it will take me 4 years to reach my goals and by that time I'll be 70 years old!"

Dave replied...
"How old will you be in 4 years if you decide not to get started in real estate investing?" **Take Action.**

I purchased more courses. Attended more seminars. Bought more books. I purchased homes, rented homes, flipped homes, rehabbed homes, But most importantly, I studied and I continued to **take action.**

My dream as a poor little boy living in a row house with my single parent father and 9 brothers & sisters was to be able to afford to visit the Haunted Mansion at Disney World.

After visiting Disney World as a young adult, my dream was to live near Disney World.

I served in the military, then went back to college, got a IT degree, then I even worked at Disney World!

Freedom to do what I want to do. Every day. That is what I wanted, and I was not willing to wait till retirement age to get it.

But what is YOUR dream?

What would you do with free time to do what you want everyday?

Get the knowledge. Hosea 4:6
Study it.   2 Timothy 2:15
Write out a plan.   Habakkuk 2:2
Take action.   Psalm 1:3

Right now real estate prices are at a all time high! So are foreclosures. Pre-foreclosures, tax sales, and sheriff sales. Bad times have always created opportunity for those who had the knowledge.

"Obstacles are those frightful things you see when you take your eyes off your goal."
- Henry Ford

"Decide, Study, Plan, Take Action"
- Brian Mahoney

"Don't wait for the right opportunity. Create it."
- George Bernard Shaw

"The only person you are destined to become is the person you decide to be."
- Ralph Waldo Emerson

Get excited! and let's begin YOUR real estate investing journey! Right Now!

PART 2:

Tax Lien and Deed Investing

1. ALL ABOUT TAX LIEN CERTIFICATE SALES

I. Sale process

In a tax lien sale, the lien (for delinquent taxes, accrued interest, and costs associated with the sale) is offered to prospective investors at public auction. Traditionally, auctions were held in person; however, Internet-based auctions (especially within large counties having numerous liens) have grown in popularity as this method allows for bidders from outside the area to participate.

In the event that more than one investor seeks the same lien, depending on state law the winner will be determined by one of five methods:

Bid Down the Interest. Under this method, the stated rate of return offered by the government is the maximum rate of return allowed. However, investors can accept lower rates of return, including zero percent in some cases (though this is rare in practice). The investor accepting the lowest rate of return is the winner. In the event more than one investor will accept the same lower rate, a random or rotational method (see below) will be used to break ties. (state and Arizona use this method)

Premium. Under this method, the investor willing to pay the highest "premium" (or excess above the lien amount) will be the winner. The premium may or may not earn interest, and may or may not be paid back to the investor upon redemption of the lien. (Colorado uses this method)

Random Selection. Under this method, a bidder will be randomly selected from those offering a bid. Usually a computer is used to make the selection, but in smaller jurisdictions more rudimentary methods may be used. Nevada uses Random selection since it is supposed to be the first buyer but it is hard to determine who was the first person to the sale.

Rotational Selection. Under this method, the first lien offered for sale will be offered to the investor holding bidder number one, who has the right of first refusal. If bidder number one refuses the lien, bidder number two may then bid. However, bidder number one will not be offered another lien until his number comes up again in the rotation. The next lien will go to the next number in line. Under this method, the investor has virtually no control over which liens s/he will obtain in the bidding, except to take or refuse what is offered.

Bid Down the Ownership. Used in IA and few other states, the investor willing to purchase the lien for the lowest percent of encumbrance on the property will be awarded the lien. For example, a bidder may agree to take a lien on only 95% of the property. If the lien is not redeemed, the investor would only receive 95% ownership of the property with the remaining 5% owned by the original owner.

In practice, few investors will bid on liens for less than full right to the property or sale proceeds.

Therefore, with multiple owners bidding on 100% encumbrance, the process then generally reverts to the random selection.

Liens not sold at auction are considered "struck" (or sold) to the entity (usually the county) conducting the auction. Some states allow "over the counter" purchases of liens not sold at auction.

II. Redemption process

The investor must wait a specified period of time (referred to as the "redemption period"), during which time the lien (plus interest and any other fees) may be repaid. Usually the lien holder is not permitted during this period to contact the property owner (or anyone else having an interest in the property, such as the mortgage holder) to demand payment or threaten foreclosure, or else the certificate can be forfeit.

In some jurisdictions, the lienholder must agree to pay subsequent unpaid property taxes during the redemption period in order to protect his/her interest. If the lienholder does not pay such taxes, a subsequent lienholder would "buy out" the prior lienholder's interest.

Once the redemption period is over, the lien holder may initiate foreclosure proceedings. The proceedings (the costs of which must be paid by the lien holder, though a redeeming property owner may be required to pay them as part of redemption) may result in either acquiring title to the property (normally this will be in the form of a quitclaim deed) or a tax deed sale of the property where the lien holder has the right of first bid (and may participate by making additional bids if s/he so chooses).

In Illinois a "Tax Deed" delivers a clean title as the court removes all clouds on title in the order directing the issuance of the deed. During the period between the initiation of proceedings and actual foreclosure, the property owner still has the opportunity to repay the lien with interest plus the costs incurred to foreclose.

If the lienholder does not act within a specified period of time, as defined by state law, the lien is forfeited and the holder loses his investment. This period of time ranges anywhere from 7 to 10 years and cannot be extended unless the taxlien is officially in the process of a tax deed application of Judicial Foreclosure.

A lien issued in error of state law is repaid, but usually at a far lower interest rate than had the lien been valid.

III. Benefits of tax lien investing

The maximum rate of return on a tax lien can be far higher than other investments. For example, one state offers a maximum rate of 18% (1.5% per month, with a guaranteed 5% return regardless of time held), while Arizona offers a maximum rate of 16%. Iowa offers a guaranteed 2% per month (or 24% annual return).

IV. Pitfalls of tax lien investing

Payment is usually required at purchase or within a very short time afterward (often no more than 24–72 hours). Failure to pay the full amount results in all lien certificates purchased by the investor being cancelled, and may result in the investor losing his/her deposit and/or being barred from future sales.

In many states, further actions must be taken to protect the lien holder's rights after purchase of a lien, and generally within a certain period of time; failure to comply exactly with such requirements may make the lien worthless.

In "bid down the interest" jurisdictions, valuable properties are usually bid to the lowest rate possible greater than zero percent. (For example, FL permits the interest rate to be bid down to a minuscule 0.25% – though it guarantees a minimum 5% return – while Arizona allows the bid to be as low as 1%.) Similarly, in "premium" states, valuable properties are bid up above the means of an average investor.

Unlike a certificate of deposit, tax liens are illiquid. They cannot be "cashed in" (resold to the taxing authority), but must be held until either they are repaid or the holder takes action to foreclose. (It is possible, however, to assign one's interest in a tax lien to another party.)

Tax Lien properties sold in non-Judicial Foreclosure states are conveyed to the highest bidder via a tax deed. The holder of the tax deed would then have to file a quiet title action, in the county where the property is situated, to clear of title defects. Although properties sold on tax deeds can be transferred, all financial institutions require a marketable title on property they will be financing.

Tax Liens that you hold on properties may become worthless due to municipal liens and assessments on the property. These liens and assessments (and their related interest) can increase the monies owed to a point that the property is deemed worthless.

2. ALL ABOUT TAX DEED SALES

A tax deed sale is the forced sale, conducted by a governmental agency, of real estate for nonpayment of taxes. It is one of two methodologies used by governmental agencies to collect delinquent taxes owed on real estate, the other being the tax lien sale.

Tax deed sale process

Real estate taxes are considered delinquent if not paid within a specified period of time. If the taxes are not paid, after legal requirements are met (such as giving proper notice to the property owner as well as others holding an interest in the property, or by filing required action in the courts), the property is offered for sale at a public auction.

At the sale, the minimum bid is generally the amount of back taxes owed plus interest, as well as costs associated with selling the property. In the event the property is not purchased, title may revert to the governmental entity that offered the property for sale. Title is generally transferred in a tax deed sale through a form of limited warranty or quitclaim deed (sometimes styled as Tax Deed or Sheriff's Deed); the purchaser would most likely then need to initiate a quiet title action in order to resell the property later (as a quitclaim deed is generally insufficient to acquire title insurance).

However, the property can be sold from one investor to another by cash or owner financing using a limited warranty, Sheriff's Deed, or even a quitclaim deed.

Some jurisdictions allow for a post-sale "redemption period," whereby the former owner has a specified amount of time to reclaim the property by repaying the amount bid at auction plus a penalty. For example, TX allows a 6-month (for non-homestead, non-agricultural properties) or two-year period (homestead or agricultural properties), with a flat 25% penalty to be added to the amount paid at the sale (50% after the first year), while Tennessee allows a full year, with a 10% penalty. As such, purchasers of properties at tax deed sales are cautioned not to make major improvements on the property until after the redemption period has expired.

A tax deed sale may also be used in conjunction with a tax lien, whereby the lienholder (instead of a governmental agency) starts the process toward forcing a public sale of the property. In those instances the lienholder's investment (the price of the lien plus any additional costs necessary to start the tax deed sale process, such as required fees and payment of any still-unpaid taxes or buyout of other certificate holders' interests) constitutes the minimum bid;

if no other bids are received at the sale then the lienholder will take title to the property subject to redemption periods (if applicable) or any lawsuit to overturn the sale (for example, failure to provide proper notice).

Section 2:

Secrets to Finding Discount Investment Property in California

Part 1:

California Real Estate Agents

It's not called show friendship, it is called show business.

When it comes to real estate agents, many now have very entertaining YouTube channels, weekend TV shows and high production commercials. You may even have a family member, church member or co-worker that dabbles in the real estate agent field. However when it comes to hiring a real estate agent, it's business. Hire the best you can find.

Here are a few traits to look for in a good real estate agent...

* Market Knowledge:

A good real estate agent has great market knowledge. They should literally have a library of properties in their head. You tell them what you want and they mention a property with little or no effort, in the price range you desire. Or can find it with relative speed.

* Not afraid to Negotiate:

You might want to negotiate their rate if you found the property or buyer yourself. They may need to negotiate on your behave, to turn a prospect into a client. They should be skilled negotiators.

* Be able to think outside the box:

Whether it is off-market deals or creative financing, they should be able to think outside the box and not be locked into average thinking, that makes other real estate agents, average.

* Availability is part of ability

It does not have to be them. As a matter of fact, many of the top real estate agents I have worked with had a team that assists them. However, somebody has to be available when the opportunity to get a deal done presents itself.

* Be able to solve common real estate investing challenges:

Top real estate agents who work with investors should have a collection of people they can recommend to you, to handle some challenges like finding a contractor, property inspector, appraiser or a property manager. Top agents usually know these people or can recommend someone who does.

* Understand Real Estate contracts

Never sign a contract without reading it. If it takes a long time, so be it. Once you have read it, a good real estate agent should be able to explain all of the provisions in the contract or get the answer in a relatively short amount of time.

* Have knowledge of Financing sources

Whether it is details about VA loans, or mortgage brokers friendly towards investors, agents should be able to assist you in one of the most important ingredients in putting a deal together. Financing.

* Be able to see the big picture

A good real estate agent should be fair, open and honest and present opportunities with the best interest of all involved in mind. And Sometimes be willing to make a little less to make a lot more. Understanding that happy customers and clients can often lead to repeat business.

A hungry monkey, will stick his hand into a peanut filled coconut shell. **It's a trap!** Once he balls up his fist, to remove the peanuts, he can no longer remove his hand from the coconut. If he would just let go of the peanuts, he could continue to live. Sadly he may lose his life, because he won't let go, of a few peanuts. Work with people who can see the bigger picture.

Select a full time real estate agent who is highly motivated and whose livelihood depends on their success. One who is experienced, with good communication skills and is flexible.

I have searched your entire state and here are 5 of the highest rated real estate agents located throughout your state.

Los angeles county   **west**
Stephanie younger group
https://stephanieyounger.com/
310 499-2020

San diego county   **south**
Team steele san diego homes
https://steelesandiegohomes.com/
619-887-4429

Sacramento county   central
Nathan sherman
http://welcometoeastsac.com/
916-969-7379

Tuolumne county   east
Pine mountain lake realty
http://www.pinemountainlakerealty.net/
209 962-7156

Siskiyou county   north
Elite real estate group
https://www.getmyhomenow.com/
530-938-0200

Remember to talk to several agents or companies, before you decide on one or maybe several agents to work with. Know what you want, why you want it and how much you are willing to pay for it. Don't let anyone else tell you what you can afford. Stay as close to what your research says as possible. Don't be afraid to walk away. AS long as you work hard on your research, you or your team will always be able to find another good deal.

Part 2:

Instant Access to a Ton of Discount Investment Property

This is where the fun starts!

There are plenty of real estate member sites, that sell the information on a monthly subscription basis, that you are about to receive from free websites. It is not hyperbole to say that the information in this chapter is worth 1,000 times what you paid for this book. I hope that... this does put a smile on your face. Because Not only am I going to give you information that gives you access to a ton of discount real estate, in your state and nationwide, but I am going to show you were you can purchase discount computers, light duty trucks, heavy duty trucks, mobile homes, motorcycles, buses, vans that a small church or small business might have need of, and much much more! All with the click of the mouse. Modern technology, it is amazing.

HUD Home Store (www.hudhomestore.com**)**

This is the government's website for HUD foreclosure homes. To purchase a Hud home you must find a hud home authorized agent. Almost every major real estate agent office has one. However you need to inquire about how many hud deals have they done. Get someone with plenty of experience.

I once had to argue with a agent who was not aware that you do not have to accept the hud listing price, but are allowed to make offers. Eventually I made a offer and they countered with a lower than listing price offer. The agent was amazed and I was sure I would shop around for a experienced hud agent the next property I purchased from them and I have purchased many.

Why is Hud one of my favorite places to purchase real estate? Banks, and governments do not have any emotional attachment to a property. Do your best to find out the debt on the property and start your bid or your offer at or below that number, depending on how much competition you believe the property will have or how bad you desire the property. I have purchased multiple homes from the government for under $10,000 dollars. I spent a lot of time doing research to find those deals and did not let a little thing like distance keep me from purchasing a home. However if you are just starting out it's a good idea to stay within 1 hour of your current residence to maximize your current knowledge of that area.

ForeclosureDataBank (www.foreclosuredatabank.com**)**

This landing page has a map of the Unites States. You click you state. Then a map of you state appears with your states cities. Click the city that you want and a list of properties appear with a photo of the property, how many bedrooms, baths, the year it was built, the square footage and the EMV the estimated market value.

To the left of the screen is a menu that allows you to show all of the properties or choose between, foreclosures, pre foreclosures, short sales or sheriff sales.

Auction.com (www.auction.com)
Enter the area were you desire a property and details of the properties appear. To include a photo, address, auction date or dates, number of bedrooms, bathes, square footage, along with the estimated resale value and the opening bid.

This site has plenty of filters that allow you to customize the properties you get to view. Options include, single family, condo, town home, multi-family and land. This website is on the list because their data base of properties is up to 3 times the size of many other websites.

Foreclosurelistings.com (www.foreclosurelistings.com)
This website takes my breath away. The landing page is a clickable map of the United States. But what makes this website special is on the left of the landing page they list the top 10 cities nationwide with the most foreclosure properties.

 If you don't like any of those cities just hit the link under the list to view more. If that was not enough, on the bottom of the page, is a list of the top 5 states and their top cites with insane nationwide numbers like... 19k short sales, 40k sheriff sales and 183k foreclosures. It may be more or it may be less when you visit this website, but the chances are... there will be plenty to choose from!

TaxSaleLists

Bid4Assets (www.bid4assets.com)
A all in one asset resource with real estate, county tax sales, sheriff's sales/foreclosures, federal, state & local government assets, U.S. Marshals Service, Bank Owned Property and $1 no reserve auctions! Auctions are categorized into real estate, art, coins, financial instruments, inventory Jewelry and Memorabilia. This landing page has a map of the United States. Simply move you mouse over your state and click to get access to your state's assets!

TaxSales.com (www.taxsales.com)
This website is an extension of the Bid4Assets website and the landing page takes you to a nationwide auction calendar
for County Tax Sales all over the United States!

TaxLiens.com (www.taxliens.com)
On the landing page of this website you enter the city, state or zip code and it gives you available properties, the
a estimate of it's rental value and the EMV which is a estimate of the properties market value.

GovDeals (www.govdeals.com)
On the landing page of this website you get a massive list of all the categories of available assets. Real Estate, SUVs, Motor Homes, Motorcycles, light & heavy duty Trucks, buses, boats, computers and much much more!

Simply hit the highlighted link of whatever it is you desire and it will take you to those items and show you
a description, location, the date the auction closes and what the current top bid is.

RealtyStore (www.realtystore.com)

Often times this website gives you the price the bank paid for a property at auction so be aware that many of the extremely low prices are for that reason. However this is valuable negotiation information as to what the bank may be willing to accept for the property.

The following is a list of bonus websites.

They are not as convenient as the other websites, but I listed them because they still may hold some value for you.

BONUS WEBSITES:

HomePath (www.homepath.com)

Fannie Mae real estate for sale. What is Fannie Mae?

The Federal National Mortgage Association, commonly known as Fannie Mae, is a United States government-sponsored enterprise and, since 1968, a publicly traded company.

This is not the easiest website to navigate but it's database is huge.

ForeclosureWarehouse (www.foreclosurewarehouse.com)
You have to join to view addresses.

TaxSaleProperty (www.taxsaleproperty.org)

These properties are in ONTARIO CANADA.

Part 3:

Wholesale Real Estate

**How to Find Wholesale Residential
& Commercial Real Estate**

How To Find Wholesale Real Estate

There are several basic methods to find real estate at wholesale prices. There are foreclosures and pre foreclosures, so get excited! There are hundreds of great deals just waiting for you to find them! The first method is Searching Public Records.

Searching Public Records

Go to your county's recorders office and look for notice of default or notice of sale. The advantage of this method is that many newly posted properties have not been seen by your competition. The disadvantage is that it usually takes more time to find property than the other methods.

Here is a tip. When ever a county clerk helps you, get that person's name and thank them face to face. Then go home and call the office and thank them again. Wait about a week. Then purchase a thank you card and mail it. Your kindness is going to stand out to that clerk. In turn that clerk is not likely to forget you. You in turn will likely have an ally in that office. The old saying "It's not what you know, but who you know." This method helps the clerk and yourself get to know each other quicker than usual. At the very least, you should feel good for being a nice person!

How To Find Wholesale Real Estate

Another advantage to searching public records is Probate Properties. You will need to be educated in your local area's probate laws to purchase those properties.

Probate is required for all estates that are not protected by a trust. The average duration of probate is 7 to 8 months.

If the house is owned outright, the estate is responsible for remitting property taxes and insurance premiums throughout the probate process.

Estate administrators can elect to sell the property if it is causing financial harm to the estate. If the estate does not have sufficient funds to cover outstanding debts, the probate judge can order the property sold.

How a probate house is sold depends on the type of probate that is used. "Court Confirmation" is the most common type of probate used. A judge must approve all of the aspects of the management of the estate. Independent Administration of Estate's Act (IAEA) governs the 2nd type of probate administration. It allows estate executors to engage in estate administrative affairs without the court management.

How To Find Wholesale Real Estate

To purchase probate property you have to know which probate system is being applied. Properties can be bought directly from the estate executor when Independent Administration of Estate's process is in effect. You can place your bid through the court system when court approval is required.

An investor interested in finding probate real estate must research public records. When people pass away their last will and testament is recorded in the probate court. The last will and testament will contain valuable information such as the estate assets, who is the beneficiary, and contact info for whoever is administrating for the estate.

Property records should show if there are any liens on the property and if so, who holds the lien. They should also show the properties appraised value, the year it was constructed, the square footage and the lot size. The records may also help you to determine if there have been any tax liens placed on the property.

Do your due diligence when purchasing any type of real estate. Bring in professional help in the form of building inspectors, lawyers and any other professionals that can help protect you when needed.

How To Find Wholesale Real Estate

Using the Internet

I will provide you with a Small Real Estate Rolodex of web sites later in this chapter. Many are completely free and have tons of information. One success algorithm for buying a property is that you should never, never, purchase one property without looking at, at least 100 other properties. Being able to search online makes using this formula very easy.

Using Local Papers and Journals

Local papers and journals. By law many foreclosures have to be posted in the local paper. This can mean a goldmine of opportunity for you. With newspaper circulation in decline, many people are simply not looking in the newspaper anymore. Advantage you.

Next I am going to cover several categories of real estate sources.

* Nationwide banks & Foreclosure Properties

* Government Foreclosure Properties

* Commercial Real Estate

* FSBO - For Sale By Owner

How To Find Wholesale Real Estate

Nationwide Banks & Foreclosure Properties

Bank of America

http://foreclosures.bankofamerica.com/

I have purchased property using this web site. It is my favorite because they have a large nationwide inventory and their web site is easy to navigate and sort properties.

Wells Fargo

https://reo.wellsfargo.com/

I placed myself on their mailing list, and get property updates on a monthly basis.

Ocwen Financial Corporation

http://www.ocwen.com/reo

Founded in 1988 they are one of the largest mortgage companies in America.

How To Find Wholesale Real Estate

Hubzu

http://www.hubzu.com/

Hubzu is a nationwide real estate auction web site. Very easy to use. This is a great web site for comparing property prices nationwide.

How To Find Wholesale Real Estate

Government Foreclosure Properties

One advantage purchasing from the government is that there is no emotional attachment to the property. Don't be afraid to make a offer that is lower than the listed price. I once argued with a real estate agent who refused to place a offer lower than the stated price. Eventually I got him to place the offer. (Remember that they work for you, however some government properties can't be purchased unless you go through a HUD or government approved agent.) It was countered twice, before I decided to purchase another property. But they countered with two offers lower than the listed price.

If you are reading a ebook version of this book then you should be able to access these web sites by clicking the links below. Buy if you are reading a paperback version of this book then be careful when looking for government properties. There are many web sites pretending to be government web sites and some will attempt to charge you fees for information about government properties.

How To Find Wholesale Real Estate

Government Foreclosure Properties

Fannie Mae
The Federal National Mortgage Association

https://www.fanniemae.com/singlefamily/reo-vendors

Department of Housing and Urban Development

https://www.hudhomestore.com/Home/Index.aspx

The Federal Deposit Insurance Corporation

https://www.fdic.gov/buying/owned/

The United States Department of Agriculture

https://properties.sc.egov.usda.gov/resales/index.jsp

United States Marshals

https://www.usmarshals.gov/assets/sales.htm#real_estate

How To Find Wholesale Real Estate

Commercial Real Estate Properties

City Feet

is a nationwide database of Commercial Real Estate Property

http://www.cityfeet.com/#

The Commercial Real Estate Listing Service

is a nationwide database of Commercial Real Estate Property

https://www.cimls.com/

Land . Net

is a nationwide database of land, commercial real estate for sale and for lease.

http://www.land.net/

Loop . Net

is a nationwide database of Commercial Real Estate Property

http://www.loopnet.com/

How To Find Wholesale Real Estate

FSBO – For Sale By Owner

By Owner

http://www.byowner.com/

For sale by owner in Canada

http://www.fsbo-bc.com/

For sale by owner Central

http://www.fsbocentral.com/

For sale by Owner: world's largest FSBO web site

http://www.forsalebyowner.com/

Ranch by owner

http://www.ranchbyowner.com/

Section 3:

How To Rehab Investment Property

Part 1:

California Handymen

One of the key members of your Real Estate Investing Team is 1 to 3 handymen or sub-contractors. In my experience you need several because if they are good, it is likely that one or more will have other jobs to do, thus putting a delay in the completion of any of your projects.

Not having a reliable handyman forced me to become fairly handy myself at fixing almost any repair. However as a businessman you learn your time is more valuable spent growing your business.

Here are a few of the advantages of having a good team of handy men.

* Keeping up with Property Maintenance

* A handyman often cost less than a professional contractors

* Regular maintenance and timely repairs keep your tenants happy and your property at it's full value.

* Keeping your property up to code and in legal compliance can keep you from costly legal issues and fines.

* Free up your time for scaling your business or spending more quality time with your family.

Now here 5 of the highest rated Handymen and Sub Contractors located throughout your state.

CALIFORNIA

1. Los angeles county   west
my handyman
https://myhandymanla.com/
424-230-3005

2. San diego county   south
unstoppable handyman
https://www.unstoppablehandyman.com/
619-729-6038

3. Sacramento county   central
honest lee handyman
https://honestleehandyman.com/
916-542-1006

4. Tuolumne county   east
dynamic handyman solutions
https://dynamichandyman.com/
209 678-9050

5. Siskiyou county   north
handymanplus services
https://www.teamhmp.com/
541-778-1365

When first starting out, don't be afraid to try several different handymen, to find out who is the most reliable in your area. Get references from family & friends as well as your local supply stores like Lowes or Home Depot.

When it comes to real estate investing, a good handyman can be worth his weight in gold.

Part 2:

A step by step guide to Rehabbing Real Estate

How to Rehab Your Property

There are three basic components to rehabbing a property. Have a property inspection, a cost analysis and hire a contractor.

A. Home Inspection

You can hire a licensed professional to inspect the property or you can do it yourself. I advise hiring a licensed professional with a great deal of experience.

To hire a professional you can google "home inspection, your city, Arizona" or go to homeadvisor.com.

http://www.homeadvisor.com/emc.Home-Inspection-directory.-12041.html

https://goo.gl/vL4gWK

If you choose to do it yourself here is a basic home inspection checklist.

Exterior

* Roof: Determine if the roof needs repairs or needs to be replaced.

* Lawn: Determine what kind of landscaping is needed or if the yard needs to be reseeded.

* Sprinkler: Is there a sprinkler system? If so does it work?

* Lights: Do the lights work? Are there motion sensors? Are they cost efficient bulbs?

* Outlets: Do the outlets work?

* Fence: Does it need repair or painting?

* Trees: Do any trees need to be removed or trimmed?

* Garage Door: Does it open and close easily?

How to Rehab Your Property

Overall Interior

* Walls: Do they need paint or repair?

* Floors: Do tiles or carpet need to be replaced? Do wood floors need to be repaired?

* Stairs: Are the stairs sturdy? Do they make noise. Is the handrail sturdy and safe?

*Outlets: Purchase a voltage tester and see if all the outlets work.

* Doors: Do they open and close easily? Are they level?

*Windows: Do you feel any breezes when you stand by them? Are they cost efficient?

*Lights: Turn on every light switch to make sure they work. (Note: If the home is unoccupied and the power is turned off, this won't be possible.)

How to Rehab Your Property

Kitchen

* **Countertops:** Check for chips and cracks.

* **Cabinets:** Do they open and close easily? Do they need to be refinished or replaced?

* **Oven:** Does the oven work? Is it outdated?

* **Refrigerator:** Check to see if it freezes. Does it pass the eyeball test or is it an eyesore.

* **Faucet:** Run the water in the sink. Any leaks? How is the water pressure?

* **Range Hood:** See if the range hood fan and light work. It most likely will need to be cleaned.

How to Rehab Your Property

Bathrooms

* Plumbing/Drainage: Fill up the sink and tub and see how the water drains out.

* Faucets: Check for leaks.

* Toilet: Is there enough pressure when it is flushed?

* Bath Tub: Is it too small? Any scratches?

* Ventilation: Does the fan work? Is there a window? Does it open and close easily?

See: Overall Interior

Bedrooms

* Closets: Is there enough space? Are hanger rods needed?

See: Overall Interior

How to Rehab Your Property

Living/Dining/Family Room

* Ceiling Fans: Do ceiling fans need to be added or replaced?

 See: Overall Interior

Basement

* Mold: If there is an odor, check for mold and mildew.

* Furnace: Does the furnace work? Is it outdated? Up to code?

* Water Heater: Check for water around the base of the water heater. Any stickers on this to indicate installation date?

A documentary about Walt Disney revealed that Walt purchased a home for his parents and a faulty gas furnace was the cause of his mother's death.

You can use this checklist to determine your offer price and begin a overall cost analysis. However it is highly recommended that you use a professional.

How to Rehab Your Property

B. Cost Analysis

When investing in real estate, you should always stack the numbers in your favor. If you can purchase a property at %50 of it's wholesale value, then you leave enough margin for error to absorb expenses and still sell the property for a profit.

The real estate web site biggerpockets.com has a investment calculator that can do the cost analysis work for you.

https://www.biggerpockets.com/real-estate-investment-calculator

https://goo.gl/HFoK9x

How to Rehab Your Property

However you can do a quick cost analysis yourself. Here are the basic numbers you will need.

* after repair value

* desired profit

* estimated repair cost

* purchase closing cost

* sale closing cost

* agent commission

* monthly holding costs

* number of days it will take to rehab and sell

Take the "after repair value" and substract all of the expenses.

C. Hire a Contractor

It is a good idea that you hire a contractor. However if you decide to do the repair work yourself there is a supply discount program from Home Depot.

WHAT IS IT?

You have to get their Pro Xtra Account. If you're spending at least $1,500, chances are you can save money. In select markets, you may only need to spend only $1,000. Check with your local store to confirm required purchase amount.

HOW DOES IT WORK?

Assemble your project list. Build your cart in the store. If your total adds up to at least $1,500 (or $1,000 in select markets, check with your local store), you probably qualify for a volume discount.

Quotes can be processed by the Pro Desk any time and most requests are priced immediately. Membership in Pro Xtra Loyalty Program is required to receive discounts.

Full details are at the web site listed below...

http://www.homedepot.com/c/Pro_VolumePricing

How to Rehab Your Property

A. How to Find a good Contractor

Go to your local building material warehouses like Lowes, Home Depot, Menards and Sherwin Williams.

Ask them who are their high volume contractors. If contractors are frequently purchasing supplies then they are frequently working. This is one of the more reliable ways to find a quality contractor.

Ask other contractors. Often times you will come across a good contractor who is busy on another project. Ask him/her for recommendations.

Ask a high volume real estate agent. Top real estate agents usually know one or two good contractors.

Use the internet.

Google "contractors, your city, Arizona".

Use homeadvisor.com

Try angieslist.com

B. Contractor Checklist

Hiring the right contractor can make or break a deal. Remember they work for you, so don't be shy about asking questions and getting proof, BEFORE you sign a contract. Here is a question checklist.

1. Do you have a license bond and insurance?

Do You Carry General Liability Insurance?

- It is Best to find a remodel contractor that carries general liability insurance

2. Do you have referrals?

Do not hesitate to call referrals. - Nice to get several customer references from the last 6 months to one year.

3. Can I get a detailed and comprehensive scope of work with the bid?

4. Ask about experience and verify if you can.

5. Who's doing the work and who's going to be the daily contact on the project?

- Make sure the contractor or his foreman is on the job whenever work is being performed.

6. Will You Pull All the Required Building Permits?

- Pulling the required building permits, you know things will be done to "code."

7. Do You Guarantee Your Work?

Your contractor should guarantee his work for at least one year from date of completion. They should also include any warranties from the material used if applicable.

8. How do you handle clean up?

Clean up can be expensive. You need to know if the best options are being used.

9. How Is Payment Handled?

- Per job?

- Upon completion?

- Weekly?

- Some money upfront?

- Do you have capital to buy materials in case we need you to?

These are basic questions that you should be asking to interview contractors before you begin any job. Hiring the right contractor can go a long way in giving you peace of mind, when you are a House Flipping Real Estate investor.

Section 4:

Fast Sale House Flipping

Part 1:

California Photographers

Real Estate Investors often underestimate the value of having a good photographer as part of your business team.

There are many benefits to investing in a top notch photographer...

High Quality Clear Images:

While it is nice to have a home that has great curb appeal in person, for many, the first time they are going to see your home is online. You never get a 2nd chance to make a first impression. So having High Quality Visuals, whether video or photographs is essential to selling or renting your investment property as soon as possible.

Increased Property Value:

Today the United States market is being flooded by buyers outside of this country. Fantastic photos and video can make the property appear more valuable then it might seem in person. This could create a bidding war, and increase the asking price. If the buyer is out of the country, your photo's or video my be all that the buyer ever sees.

Staging Assistance:

Having a house properly staged and photographed can make all the difference in the perceived value of the investment property. A professional photographer with plenty of experience can spot, and remove the little details that can turn a buyer or renter away.

Expanding your Audience Reach:

With great photography and video content you can expand your property pass the traditional websites like Zillow and Realtor.com. Social media showings have become quite popular on YouTube and other social media platforms. Attracting a wider audience of potential buyers and renters.

These are just a few of the benefits of having a professional real estate photographer added to your business team.

Now here are 5 of the top rated photographers in located throughout your state.

CALIFORNIA

1. Los angeles county   **west**
visual open house
https://www.visualopenhouse.com/
323-365-6109

2. San diego county   **south**
greg hoxsie photography
https://sandiegorealestatephotographer.pro/
808-298-7244

3. Sacramento county   **central**
legacy images
https://saclegacyimages.com/
916-957-6424

4. Tuolumne county   **east**
thompson real estate media
https://www.thompsonrealestatephoto.com/
209-250-7726

5. Siskiyou county   **north**
redding real estate photography
http://www.reddingrephoto.com/
530-949-2444

Remember, having a professional real estate photographer can give you a huge competitive advantage and can reduce the days your property sits on the market, as well as enhance and professionalize your company's brand image. The reduced cost of having the property on the market for less time, just might be more than enough to justify the cost of a professional photographer.

Part 2:

House Flipping

Introduction to House Flipping

House Flipping is a type of real estate investment strategy in which an investor purchases properties with the goal of reselling them for a profit. Profit is generated by purchasing a property well under market value, through the property appreciation in a good housing market or from renovations and capital improvements that increase the value of the investment.

If you want to use the House Flipping real estate investment strategy there a few things you need to do to be successful.

1. Get Knowledge

"My people are destroyed for lack of knowledge..." Hosea 4:6

This book is a beginning. Throughout this book there will be links placed for you to get more education. In addition, there is a web Rolodex resource section near the end this book, that has more real estate sources to bolster your education.

The "Real Estate Terms" section at the end of this book will also help in getting you caught up to the real estate lingo used by real estate professionals.

Introduction to House Flipping

2. Secure Financing

I was at a real estate seminar and the instructor asked "what's worth more, a house worth $100,000 or $100,000 cash"? Many people in the audience said "The house. It will appreciate in value." The instructor replied "The $100,000 in cash. With that I can buy the house." If you are going to be an investor, the first thing you need to do is know where or how you are going to finance your business.

You are going to need money to purchase a property and to repair it. There are several sources for funding.

* Your personal savings

* A credit card

* Bank loan

* Hard & Private Money Lenders

* Partners

* Investors

* Family and Friends

More funding details in chapters 3 and 4.

3. Begin with then end in mind.

Write a business plan. Set a budget. Choose a specialty.

Begin with the end in mind. A business plan helps you to chart a course of action. Having a business plan can also help you to secure money from a financial institution.

Set a budget. People who lose money in real estate either don't have a budget or don't stick to one. A friend once asked me to finance a property. I asked for the address. I looked at the property and the asking price. Within 24 hours I found a property in the same area that was %50 less and equal in quality. I found that property in part because I had a budget set, and was not willing to go over it. Other people will be more than happy to spend your money and tell you what you can afford. You need to know what you can and can't afford before you get started.

Introduction to House Flipping

Choose a specialty. There are plenty to choose from...

* Residential Property

* Commercial Property

* Apartments

* Duplexes

* 3 bedroom homes

* Mobile Homes

* Government Properties

* Bank Properties

* Probate Properties

Learn all you can about a real estate niche, and stick to it until you become very proficient.

4. Find a great property.

One of the reasons finding a property at a great wholesale price is possible is because many people skip step 2: securing financing. When I was purchasing properties from the government, I learned that cash had priority in many of the deals, even if I was offering less than the asking price.

Risk is a necessary component of success. Purchasing from the government is a great way to get started because there is less risk involved. There are weasels in every business. In general the government is less interested in making a profit and more concerned with getting rid of a non performing asset.

Moving a non-performing asset, is also the same mindset for many banks. There is less emotional value attached to a property as opposed to buying from a regular home owner.

Part of finding a great property is reducing risk. Sticking with the government or banks might reduce your profit, but if you are new to real estate investing, then it is good to get a couple of deals under your belt to build confidence and gain experience.

5. Put Together a Team

Your team should include but not be limited to...

* a few experienced real estate agents

* a few good contractors and sub-contractors

* a good place to purchase supplies

* a real estate attorney

* a title company

* an accountant

There is enough basic information here to get you started, but we are going to cover in more detail many of the topics mentioned in this introduction.

I once purchased a 3 bedroom house from the government for $1,500. Recently a bank sold me a 5 bedroom house for under $10,000 with a .6 acre (that's the size of an NFL Football Field) back yard in a quiet neighborhood.

Was it Luck?

Introduction to House Flipping

"**Luck** Is What Happens When **Preparation** Meets Opportunity"

Seneca

While I was taking classes and running an online business, I spent 3 hours a day, 5 days a week going through real estate web sites looking for deals.

If you are serious about making money in real estate then treat real estate investing like a business not a hobbie. Part time effort produces part time results.

The longest journey begins with one step.

"Inch by inch, life's a cinch. Yard by yard, life's hard."

— John Bytheway

Part 3:

How to Sell Your Investment Property Fast!

HOW TO SELL YOUR PROPERTY FAST!

12 Steps to Selling Any Property Fast!

1. Clean and Paint the house

Make sure the house is clean and uncluttered. This makes it easier for a buyer to envision themselves living there. Make the bathrooms and kitchen a priority.

2. Scent the house

You might use a light incent or get some vanilla extract and place it on a old school lightbulb to give it a fresh baked cookie smell.

3. Write a property description

Writing a great property description is key to getting buyers interested in your home. One short cut to learning how to write a good property description is to view property listings of sold properties.

4. Take Good pictures

If you don't have a good camera, buy one. A picture is worth a 1,000 words.

HOW TO SELL YOUR PROPERTY FAST!

12 Steps to Selling Any Property Fast!

5. **Send a email to your buyers list**

If you do not have a buyer's list, here is a link to a complete set of training videos on how to build a valuable customer list.

https://urlzs.com/6Q2uQ

6. Post ads on craigslist

Keep reposting your ads on a daily basis so that you stay at the top of the search results.

7. Post ads to Backpage

http://www.backpage.com/

This is a Worldwide Classified Ad Web Site.

HOW TO SELL YOUR PROPERTY FAST!

12 Steps to Selling Any Property Fast!

8. Place a Ad on http://realeflow.com/

This is the number one source for real estate investing leads.

9. visit the zillow rental manager https://www.zillow.com/rental-manager/

This is a free rental web site.

10. Create a video virtual tour

Create a video virtual tour and upload the video to YouTube. This is a powerful tool. YouTube is 2nd only to Google as the largest Search Engine in the world. However just posting a video won't get it seen. It has to be Search Engine Optimized(SEO). Below is a link to training videos that will show you step by step how to create great videos and get massive traffic viewing them!

https://urlzs.com/6Q2uQ

HOW TO SELL YOUR PROPERTY FAST!

12 Steps to Selling Any Property Fast!

11. Post an ad on facebook target a city

You can place an ad on Facebook and target the city that your property is in.

12. Place a Standard For Sale sign in the yard

If possible have flyers available as well.

13. Place addition white signs in the yard

Give more information and get more attention by placing more personal signs in the yard.

14. List the property in the MLS

If you are not a real estate agent get one to do it for you.

15. Place directional signs

Help people find your house. Make sure you are not violating any county codes when placing signs.

16. Continue marketing until closing

Don't slack off. If necessary you might want to hire VA's Virtual Assistants to keep all ads running.

17. Eliminating Negative Cash Flow

https://www.airbnb.com/

Airbnb is a web site that markets your house or rooms in your house for rent. It's easier to sell your house when it is clean, empty and buyers can envision themselves living in it.

However, if you are suffering from negative cash flow you might want to look into just renting out 1 room in the house.

HOW TO SELL YOUR PROPERTY FAST!
12 Steps to Selling Any Property Fast!

In Summary

1. Clean and Paint the house

2. Scent the house

3. Write a property description

4. Take Good pictures

5. Send a email to your buyers list

6. Post ads on craigslist

7. Post ads to http://www.backpage.com/

8. Place a Ad on http://realeflow.com/

9. https://www.zillow.com/rental-manager/

10. Create a video virtual tour

11. Post an ad on facebook target a city

12. Place a Standard For Sale sign in the yard

13. Place addition white signs in the yard

14. List property in the MLS

15. Place directional signs

16. Continue marketing until closing

17. Rent on Airbnb to eliminate negative cashflow

Take these steps to sell your property and you stack the odds in your favor for a quick property sale!

Section 5:

Conclusion

Congratulations for finishing the **California** Tax Lien and Deed Investing Book. You now have the knowledge to start your business, and put in the work, and give yourself the opportunity to live the Hassle Free
All-American Lifestyle of Independence, Prosperity and Peace of Mind.

You now have discovered...

* The benefits of Tax Lien or Deed Investing in **California**

* How to Find the best Tax Lien or Deed and Wholesale Real Estate in **California**

* The top Real Estate Investing Agents, Handymen & photographers in **California**

* The top Handymen and Sub Contractors in your state

* How to Find the best Tax Lien or Deed and Wholesale Real Estate for Nationwide Investing

* How to Find Wholesale Land, SUVs, Mobile Homes, & more from the Government

* All about Wholesale Real Estate Investing Strategy

* How to Rehab Real Estate Investment Property Step by Step

* A "How to" Guide to Flipping a House

* How to Sell your Investment Property... Fast!

and Much Much More!

"An investment in knowledge pays the best interest."
Benjamin Franklin

To be successful, it takes more than knowledge, you
have to take proper **action!**

"And he shall be like a tree planted by the rivers of
water, that bringeth forth his fruit in his season; his
leaf also shall not wither; and **whatsoever he
doeth** shall prosper." **Psalm 1:3**

Now get excited! and let's begin your investing
journey! Right Now!

"You don't have to be great to start, but you have to
start to be great." - Zig Ziglar

Finally, if you enjoyed this book, please take the time to share your thoughts and post a review on Amazon. It'd be greatly appreciated!

Many Thanks,

Brian Mahoney

We want to thank you for the purchase of this book and more importantly, thank you for reading it to the end. We hope your reading experience was pleasurable and that you would inform your family and friends on Facebook, Twitter or other social media.

We would like to continue to provide you with high-quality books, and that end, would you mind leaving us a review on Amazon.com?

Just use the link below, scroll down about 3/4 of the page and you will see images similar to the one below.

We are extremely grateful for your assistance. Warm Regards, MahoneyProducts Publishing

Book Link:

Customer reviews

4.6 out of 5 stars   4.6 out of 5
6 global ratings

5 star   64%_
4 star   36%-
3 star 0% (0%)   0%
2 star 0% (0%)   0%
1 star 0% (0%)
Review this product
Share your thoughts with other customers

(Write a Customer Review)

You might also enjoy:

How To Get Money for Small Business Start Up: How to Get Massive Money from Crowdfunding, Government Grants and Government Loans

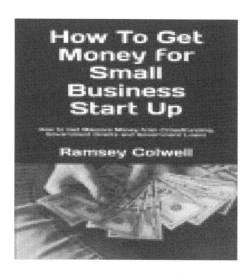

https://www.amazon.com/dp/1951929144

Want Free Books to Review?

Join Our VIP Mailing List Then Get Notified when we release our new books on FREE promotions.

FREE Amazon ebooks and free Audible ACX audio books!

Just click or Type in the Link Below

https://urlzs.com/HfbGF

Made in the USA
Columbia, SC
30 November 2023

27436301R00057